INTERRUPTED LIVES

INTERRUPTED LIVES

Nine Stories *of* Child Survivors *of* the Holocaust

EDITED by AMANDA FRIEDEMAN
and KELLEY SZANY

KAR-BEN
PUBLISHING

For all the survivors. Thank you for your strength, courage, and resilience, reminding us of the need to remember the past in order to transform the future. —A.F. and K.S.

ILLINOIS HOLOCAUST MUSEUM & EDUCATION CENTER

In association with the Illinois Holocaust Museum & Education Center and Biograph LLC. The stories collected here are based on interviews with the survivors conducted in 2018 by Aaron and AJ Greenberg.

KAR-BEN PUBLISHING®
An imprint of Lerner Publishing Group, Inc.
241 First Avenue North
Minneapolis, MN 55401 USA

Website address: www.karben.com

Interior and cover photos courtesy of: Adele Zaveduk, p. 9; Barney Sidler, p. 16; Zachor the Holocaust Memory Project, p. 22; Eric Blaustein, p. 25; Ernst K. Heimann, p. 31; the Stern family, pp. 35, 38, 60, 65; Judy Straus, p. 45; IHMEC: courtesy of Magda Brown, p. 48; Rodi Glass, pp. 54, 56. Portrait photos copyright © by John Pregulman/KAVOD, pp. 6, 14, 28, 40, 47.

Main body text set in Adobe Garamond Pro. Typeface provided by Adobe Systems.

Library of Congress Cataloging-in-Publication Data

Names: Friedeman, Amanda, editor. | Szany, Kelley, editor.
Title: Interrupted lives : nine stories of child survivors of the Holocaust / edited by Amanda Friedeman, and Kelley Szany.
Other titles: Nine stories of child survivors of the Holocaust
Description: Minneapolis : Kar-Ben Publishing, [2025] | Audience: Ages 10–15 | Audience: Grades 5–9 | Summary: "After surviving World War II and the Holocaust as children, nine survivors share their memories in first-person interviews" —Provided by publisher.
Identifiers: LCCN 2024008832 | ISBN 9798765607763 (paperback) | ISBN 9798765662656 (epub)
Subjects: LCSH: Holocaust survivors—Interviews. | Jewish children in the Holocaust—Europe—Interviews—Juvenile literature. | Holocaust, Jewish (1939–1945)—Europe—Juvenile literature. | World War, 1939–1945—Atrocities—Juvenile literature.
Classification: LCC D804.48 .I584 | DDC 940.53/180922—dc23/eng/20240226

LC record available at https://lccn.loc.gov/2024008832

Manufactured in the United States of America
2-1012456-51424-8/25/2025

CONTENTS

BIRTH: *August 4, 1937*
HOMETOWN: *Paris, France*
HOLOCAUST EXPERIENCE: *Hidden child*
LIBERATION DATE: *1945*
IMMIGRATION TO AMERICA: *1963*
DEATH: *January 23, 2020*

ADELE ZAVEDUK

Accept and Try to Reconcile

I started talking about my Holocaust experience in 1985. We were gathered at the synagogue for *Shabbat*—the Jewish day of rest. The synagogue asked three ladies to discuss their upbringing. I would usually say no when asked to talk about my youth, but on that day I said yes.

I was a little girl in France at the beginning of World War II. I have no recollections of Jewish life in France before the war. My mother never talked about our Jewishness, perhaps to protect us. Children repeat what they hear at home, and at that time, it could have meant the difference between life and death. My father was already a prisoner in Drancy.

I remember that my mother wore a yellow star on her coat. I couldn't understand why she tried to cover it with her purse.

In 1941, through an underground Jewish agency, my mother placed my sister and me with the Mullards, a Catholic family living in a small town in central France. As a mother, I now realize how difficult it must have been for her to give up her children. But she knew the Nazis were rounding up Jews; women and children were immediately being shipped to the death camps.

Madame Mullard denounced my mother. The police came, and my mother was forced to take the train back to Paris. She didn't say goodbye to us. She didn't give us a reason why she was leaving. She just disappeared. On her return to Paris, she was picked up and sent to Drancy—and then to Auschwitz.

Madame Mullard told us our mother had abandoned us because she was a bad woman. What is a bad woman to a five-year-old? My sister, Josette, and I had no idea. Our mother had left us. Period.

We lived with Madame Mullard. She treated us like her own children. She shared everything with us: food, clothing, shelter—and her Catholic religion. Reading my catechism was no problem because

What Was Drancy?

Drancy was an internment camp established by the Germans in August 1941 north of Paris, in a suburb called Drancy. By the following summer, it was the major transit camp for deportations of Jews from France. Prisoners would be held at Drancy for short periods, often just days or weeks. The majority of Jewish people imprisoned at Drancy were sent to Auschwitz-Birkenau and murdered.

What Was Auschwitz?

Located in German-occupied Poland, Auschwitz consisted of three concentration camps including a killing center at Birkenau. Over 1.1 million people were murdered at Auschwitz, including nearly 1 million Jews. Operational in 1942, Auschwitz III (Buna-Monowitz) eventually became the center of the Auschwitz network of more than forty forced-labor camps. In January 1945, the Soviet army liberated Auschwitz.

I had no memories of an earlier religion. Josette and I were like two typical Catholic country girls.

Because it was wartime, you needed a coupon to buy shoes or clothes. While Madame Mullard had coupons, she didn't have money. She and her daughter used to go to people's houses to wash their laundry. The people were nice. When their children's clothes became too small, they would give them to Madame Mullard. Those became our clothes. A neighbor would take pieces of wood and carve us clogs, which we wore during the winter. We didn't have socks, so we'd wrap our feet in newspaper.

Once a week, we had to take a bath. We would bathe in an aluminum tub. There were six of us. The first one in would have clean water. Number six's water—well, it wasn't so clean.

I went to school in the little town for five years. The Germans did not have control over the town, but every so often, Nazis would come in a Jeep, drive around, and leave. No one had owned a car—even if they had, there was no gasoline. The people in town traveled by horse and buggy.

When the Germans stopped by the school, the teacher would order a few of us to go play outside and not come back until she sent someone to get us. The soldiers would come in asking for the Jews, and she would say, "No, we don't have any Jews here." It took me years to realize how brave those teachers were. If the soldiers had found us, they would have shot us, the teacher, and Madame Mullard. I never thanked my teachers for their bravery. There is no way to thank them.

Adele as a young girl

Once, the Germans came to our house. Madame Mullard hid me, my sister, and a little Jewish boy named Joseph under the bed, covered by a blanket. Madame Mullard told the Germans that we kids had chicken pox—which was true. One of us did. "They're contagious," Madame Mullard warned. The German soldiers turned around and left. They never entered the room. We were saved by chicken pox that day.

People in the town knew that we were Jews. It's amazing that nobody turned us in. I learned later that there were nine Jewish children hidden there at the time. When the Germans came, some people were denounced, and some Jewish children were taken away—but not us.

Almost four years later, in late 1945, both my parents returned to Paris after being liberated from the concentration camps. The United Nations Relief and Rehabilitation Administration (UNRRA) reunited us. Once again, we became a family. There were, however, some problems. When my parents came back from the concentration camps, they were not the same as they had been. They loved us and took care of us, but something was missing.

I was angry because I didn't understand why my mother had left us. It took me many years to get over that. For a year, I never let my mother touch me. My mother would go out and try to find nice things, like bananas, for my sister and me. She would give each of us a banana, but I wouldn't eat mine. I thought I would have preferred that she took us with her when she left for the concentration camp, but eventually, I learned that we wouldn't have lasted twenty-four hours in the camp.

My sister and I had no memories of these strangers being our parents. I didn't believe they were my mother and father. When we were separated, I was only four years old and my sister was two. Now, I was an eight-year-old Catholic girl with a Jewish mother and father. I think about my parents' reaction to this, especially after the price they had paid for being Jews.

At school, during recess, I would ask my friends to teach me what they had learned that Sunday in church. I dreamed about my first Communion. "Jewish girls don't do Communion," Momma used to say. I brought crosses home from school, and she would throw them away, but she never explained why.

My mother kept the Sabbath and the holidays, but neither Momma nor Poppa taught us about Judaism. I had no Jewish friends or relatives in Paris. My parents were the only survivors of what had once been a large family.

A few of my parents' friends who had survived would get together and talk about the Holocaust. When the adults didn't want us to understand, they would speak Yiddish, but most of the conversations were in French. I would listen, and little by little, I started to learn. Even though I was ten and naive, their words stayed in my mind.

I was fourteen when I left France. I didn't want to go. My mother had two brothers and a sister who had immigrated to Argentina long before the war. In 1950, my parents decided to join them in Buenos Aires. Our family now included a two-year-old brother born after the war. Unfortunately, my father died before we could leave. With my mother and two siblings, I left France forever.

The Jewish community of Buenos Aires was my first real introduction to Judaism. I enjoyed it, but I never felt I was part of the community. When I was seventeen, my mother remarried. My stepfather was an Orthodox Jew—observing Jewish law was the focus of his days. Suddenly, I found myself living in a kosher home. We strictly observed all the dietary laws of the Torah, including no shellfish or pork. I had difficulty adjusting, and I often accidentally mixed up the dishes because it was not important to me. My stepfather would rise in the morning and pray, which I thought was nonsense. Yet I had been raised not to challenge but to accept. In spite of myself, I started to learn about Judaism, more as a sign of respect to my mother than as a believer.

As a teenager, all my friends were Jews. I went to temple on all the holidays. However, most of the temples in Buenos Aires were Orthodox. I didn't feel comfortable when I attended. I was used to going to Mass. My first time at a synagogue was on a Jewish holiday. I didn't understand any of the prayers. There were kids running around, people dancing and celebrating. I thought to myself, "This is the Jewish religion? It's chaos."

There was freedom of religion in Argentina, and there was an active Jewish community. However, antisemitism was widespread. I had to live with it every day. What I had accepted as a child was now unbearable. Occasionally, graffiti appeared on public walls that read in Spanish: *Be patriotic. Kill a Jew.*

My husband, Benjamin, was born into a Jewish family in Argentina. When our first child was born, we decided that Argentina was no place to raise him. So we left for the United States and settled in Oak Park, Illinois. We joined a Reform temple, but I could not identify with the congregation. We joined a Conservative synagogue. This changed everything. My acceptance by the congregation made me feel one with the Jewish community.

"I am a woman who has lived Jewish history and survived its darkest hour," I tell people. "I am surrounded by my friends at the synagogue. I keep a Jewish home and raise my two children to understand and love their heritage. I have finally become a Jew."

I realize that people categorize me as a survivor, but I've never felt like a survivor. I didn't suffer like those in concentration camps. My mother and father were survivors. They had numbers on their arms. My life was different. I was playing outside while they were in the camps.

My life was interrupted, but I didn't realize it. When you are five years old, it doesn't bother you to live in a house with six barefoot kids and to wear somebody else's old clothes. I suffered in a different way from many Holocaust survivors. I suffered separation. I suffered culture shock. I suffered religious shock—which lingered long after we defeated the Nazis. I had been comfortable being Catholic and struggled to adjust.

For a long time, my mother never spoke about her war experience. Eventually, though, she taped her testimony. "Mother, why didn't you tell us about your experiences?" I asked afterward.

"I didn't want to burden you with what happened to us," she said. "And why didn't you ask me about it?"

"I didn't want to bring back painful memories," I said. We were covering for each other, trying not to hurt each other, but that was wrong. If someone in the family would have asked, she would have answered. By the time she gave her testimony, I was a grown woman, and many opportunities for understanding had been lost.

Now I often share my story. I tell my story because many children have it tough too. I teach them that you can overcome what has happened to you. You cannot live with bitterness.

ADELE'S LESSON:
Accept and Try to Reconcile

Adele's story emphasizes acceptance—but not without understanding. Her story teaches us to distinguish between circumstances we should accept and those we should not accept. She had been raised not to challenge rules, but that sometimes caused her great pain. For example, she struggled to readjust to being a Jew after years of living as a Catholic. But her struggles with faith, identity, and family finally led her to understand—although perhaps not forgive—her mother's actions and to embrace her own Judaism. Adele came to accept that her mother's decision to leave her was motivated by love, which ultimately saved Adele's life. And eventually, Adele found a Jewish community that supported and welcomed her.

BIRTH: *March 1933*
HOMETOWN: *Dęblin, Poland*
HOLOCAUST EXPERIENCE: *Concentration camp survivor*
LIBERATION DATE: *April 11, 1945*
IMMIGRATION TO AMERICA: *1950*

BARNEY SIDLER

Try to Be Optimistic in Life

I was six years old when the war came to my hometown of Dęblin, Poland. In October 1939, the government ordered that all Jews wear white armbands with blue Stars of David. If you didn't wear an armband, you could be arrested or even shot.

In March 1940, my family and I were sent to the ghetto. I had to leave the first grade, as Jews could no longer go to school. Jews were forced from their homes and moved into cramped apartments in the ghetto; there were ten of us living in a three-room apartment with no bathroom. The non-Jewish Poles who lived in this area moved into the apartments and houses the Jews had vacated.

A Jewish council (*Judenrat*) was formed, as well as a Jewish police force. The council's job was to ensure that Nazi orders and rules were enforced in the ghetto. The council was made up of twelve elderly, prominent, and respected Jewish men. My dad was on the council, and his job included reporting to the Nazis what was going on in the ghetto.

In 1941, the Nazis began "roundups" in the ghetto, arresting Jews and deporting them to killing centers in the East. In early May 1942, there was a big deportation in our ghetto. Over a thousand Jews were sent to Sobibor. I remember watching mothers carrying babies in their arms. The Nazis took the children from the mothers and often killed the children. Seeing the murder of these infants, I wept.

What Were the Ghettos?

The Nazi government isolated and contained Jews within specific areas of cities called ghettos. Surrounded by barbed wire or walls, the ghettos were often sealed, separating Jews from the non-Jewish population. Established mostly in occupied eastern Europe, the ghettos were characterized by overcrowding, starvation, and forced labor.

What Was the Judenrat?

Most ghettos had a Judenrat, the German word for "Jewish Council." It was made up of respected Jewish men selected by the Nazis. The Judenrat was created to make sure that all the Nazi laws were enforced in the ghetto. The council reported to the Nazis about what was going on in the ghetto and, in some cases, even helped in the selection of Jews to be taken to concentration camps.

Barney, *center*, as a young child with family members

Three months later, a second large deportation took place, with the Nazis deporting almost all the Jews who remained in the ghetto. The only people left were agricultural workers, laborers at the airport, the Jewish police, and the council members—so my family and I were spared since my father was on the council. Perhaps we also survived because of a little luck.

Because Dęblin was a strategic city, major trains ran through it. We saw many transports of Jews—and we had no illusions about their fate.

In 1944, I was deported, along with all the Jews left in the city, to the Częstochowa concentration camp. I was

What Was Sobibor?

Sobibor was a Nazi killing center in occupied eastern Poland. The camp was established in March 1942 and shut down at the end of 1943 after a prisoners' uprising. About 250,000 Jews were killed at Sobibor.

assigned to kitchen duty. My job was sorting the good potatoes from the rotten potatoes. I'd wear two pairs of baggy pants so that I could steal potatoes. My mother would cook them and add them to our soup. If I had been caught, I could have been put in solitary confinement or even executed.

What Was Częstochowa?

First established as a ghetto, Częstochowa became a forced labor camp. The labor was used in the city's armament factories, which belonged to a privately owned German industrial company.

Every day in the camp was the same. It was miserable. But I got used to it. Every morning, the Nazis would count us to make sure that nobody had escaped—and to see if anyone had died. The dead were thrown on the ground in front of the barracks and then buried in a mass grave.

After about three months in the camp, the Nazis requested that all Jews go to the *Appelplatz*, the place for daily roll calls. My brother tried to escape and was caught. The Germans took him to the center of town to punish him as an example of what could happen to those who tried to escape, but he escaped again and ran to a Polish church. The priest hid him in a casket for ten days. He came back to the camp using the name of someone who had died two days earlier.

In January 1945, I was transported to Buchenwald. It took ten days.

There were hundreds of people per railcar, with no toilet facilities. Some people drank urine to satisfy their thirst. We were not given food, and many people died.

When we arrived, the Nazis threw our belongings into a big barrel. Then they told us to undress and take showers. We all had heard what that meant—gas chambers!—so when we filed into

What Was Buchenwald?

One of the first Nazi concentration camps, Buchenwald opened in 1937 near Weimar, Germany. It held Jews, political prisoners, and Romani, among others. Prisoners worked as forced laborers in local armament factories. More than fifty-six thousand people were murdered at Buchenwald.

the shower room and, to our surprise, saw water running, we danced, cried, and kissed one another.

In Buchenwald, I befriended a German doctor. He had been imprisoned because he was anti-Hitler. "You remind me of my son," he told me, and he offered to help me. Being a doctor, he had a small cottage in the camp. He hid me in a laundry basket filled with dirty towels. "Do you have a Jew?" the German Gestapo would ask him "No. No Jews here," the doctor would lie. With those words he saved my life.

I was in Buchenwald for four months. My brother was transported to another camp four weeks before liberation. I was told that he hid in a barn that was burned down by the Germans. My father was still with me. He kept reminding me that I had an uncle in Chicago. He kept making me repeat his name and address. Two days before liberation, my father was marched into a nearby forest and shot. I was liberated on April 11, 1945. There were 156 people in my family before the war; only 10 of us survived.

At twelve, I was one of the youngest survivors of Buchenwald, and my picture ran in many newspapers.

After liberation, a Jewish chaplain came to me and asked if I wanted to go to the United States. He told me I would be placed in an orphanage. I said no. "I left my mother and two sisters behind in Częstochowa," I said. "I am not an orphan until I find out if any of my family is still there."

The Hebrew Immigrant Aid Society (HIAS) paid for a train ticket for me back to my hometown.

After two hours waiting on the platform, I heard a train coming from the direction of my hometown, Dęblin. Suddenly, I heard someone shout, "Barry!"—which was my Polish name. It was my cousin Howard. He had heard that my mother and sister had gone to Lublin. So we left for Lublin. Howard told me that somebody from Buchenwald had told my mother that I had been killed. She didn't know I had survived.

"We can't just walk in on your mother," he said. "We need to prepare her." So, while I stayed with my relatives for a week, the American Red Cross sent a letter to my mother telling her I was alive and would be coming to town. She cried. I learned then that my other sister had moved to Israel with her husband, and three months later we received word from the Red Cross that my brother had also survived! He would join us in a few weeks.

At the age of twelve, I was the breadwinner. I earned money on the black market to support my family. I bought my mother oranges, bananas, cheesecake, chocolate, and doughnuts—the little luxuries she craved that she said kept

What Is the Hebrew Immigrant Aid Society?

HIAS was established in the United States in 1881 to help Jewish immigrants and refugees. After World War II, many Jews and others were living in displaced persons camps in Europe. HIAS helped resettle about 150,000 people in 330 communities in the United States, Canada, Australia, and countries in South America. HIAS is still a global Jewish humanitarian organization that helps refugees find welcome, safety, and opportunity.

her feeling human. In 1946, we moved to Łódź, Poland, where I earned money by selling theater tickets on the black market.

The antisemitism in Poland became so bad that we decided to leave for Germany with the help of HIAS. We lived in a displaced persons camp there for about a year.

Dr. David Friedman in Norfolk, Virginia, sponsored my brother and me to come to the United States. We left Hamburg, Germany, and arrived at Ellis Island in New York City. When we landed, the person from HIAS said that my uncle had seen my picture in the newspaper! "He saw that you were one of the children who was liberated from Buchenwald. He wants you to come."

Originally, my surname was Einschidler, but in the United States, my aunt advised me to cut the name short. "It's going to be easier. If anybody asks you how to spell your name, you say, 'You know how to spell *fiddler*? Take the F away. Put an S in front.' So now I'm Barney Sidler."

When I arrived in Chicago at the age of sixteen, I stayed with my uncle for a while. He sent me to a private school to learn English. He also got me a job making venetian blinds. I had only spent three months in first grade before the Nazis came. The only English words I could say were "yes," "no," and "thank you."

I started telling my story at eighteen. I wanted other people to know what I suffered and what I accomplished. I always looked forward. It was not easy. I prayed. I hoped that I would survive. I never gave up.

BARNEY'S LESSON:
Try to Be Optimistic in Life

Barney faced unimaginable hardships at a very young age. His ability to remain optimistic—to believe that things would turn out okay despite everything he saw and experienced—was critical to his survival. His positive attitude, including always looking forward while never forgetting his past, allowed him to build a good life with a loving family and a successful career.

BIRTH: *September 19, 1926*
HOMETOWN: *Chemnitz, Germany*
HOLOCAUST EXPERIENCE: *Hidden in the open; concentration camp survivor*
LIBERATION DATE: *April 16, 1945*
IMMIGRATION TO AMERICA: *1954*

ERIC BLAUSTEIN
Play Your Part

I am not your typical Holocaust survivor. I spent only a little time in a concentration camp. I did not suffer as others suffered. I was born in Chemnitz, Germany, on September 19, 1926, into an assimilated Jewish family. My mother was a dressmaker. My father was a public accountant.

Until 1938, things were unpleasant but bearable. We had an apartment. My father had enough money. I was ostracized at school. Then, on November 9, 1938—*Kristallnacht*, or "The Night of Broken Glass"—my father was arrested and sent to a concentration camp.

We watched as the Germans burned the town synagogue. Much later, I learned that thousands of synagogues were burned down that night and thirty thousand men were sent to concentration camps.

At age fifteen, I was out on a Sunday tending my vegetable garden when the town gravedigger, who had once been a lawyer, approached me. His arm was in a sling. "The Nazis want me to dig some graves," he said. "Can you help me? I broke my arm." Things were so bad that we did what had to be done. I dug those two graves for him. Soon after, the Nazis arrested the gravedigger and sent him to a concentration camp.

What Was Kristallnacht?

On November 9, 1938, the Nazis unleashed a pogrom—a violent riot targeting Jewish homes, businesses, and synagogues—on Jewish communities in Germany, Austria, and the Sudetenland, a German-speaking region of Czechoslovakia. About seventy-five hundred Jewish-owned businesses, homes, and schools were plundered, 267 synagogues were burned or destroyed, and ninety-one Jews were murdered. An additional thirty thousand Jewish men were arrested and sent to concentration camps. Kristallnacht, or "The Night of Broken Glass," refers to the broken windows of synagogues, stores, and homes.

Food was in short supply. I worked twelve-hour days, loading bodies into a two-wheeled cart and pushing it to the cemetery. I buried many people.

When I was nearly sixteen, one of my father's friends came to our house and warned my mother that I was in danger. So from 1941 to 1944, I lived underground. I had papers that identified me as a Hitler Youth leader. I could say "*guten Tag*" and click my heels like a German officer. My fake papers were not convincing. The first time I had to show them, the guy looked at them, looked at me, and asked if I was kidding. Still, those papers got me through some tight situations.

It became normal for me to move to a new house every couple of weeks. I was allowed to travel on the pretense of visiting Hitler Youth organizations in other cities. I relied on strangers to feed and clothe me. I tried to make myself small enough to not inconvenience or aggravate my hosts in any way. I had to be careful. But it was better than being in a concentration camp.

I hid for about five months in a library, educating myself in German literature. I hid in the home of a retired World War I general. I hid in the home of Communists. I hid in the home of a religious Christian. Their motives for helping me were different, but they all felt that something was wrong and that they needed to help.

I grew antennas during that time. I had to. When I met people, I had to figure out quickly: Are you a good German or a bad German? Will you turn me in, or will you help me?

On September 19, 1944, my birthday, a man ordered me to identify myself as I went to buy a newspaper. He thought I was a deserter from the army. I knew the Nazis hung deserters to make an example of them, but that, by law, they had to send Jews to concentration camps. "I am not a deserter," I told him. "I'm a Jew."

He was shocked. "What Jew is still alive in Germany?!" he asked.

The authorities sent me to Buchenwald. Some inmates saved my life the moment I arrived. "The kapo will kill you tomorrow. They kill any Jew who arrives here," they told me. So they quickly swapped my identity number with that of an Italian fellow, Luigi, who was a bit older than me and had just died. The next morning at roll call, the guards took Luigi's body out and pronounced Eric Blaustein dead. I was Luigi after that.

Because I spoke German well, several guards had the idea that I should become the interpreter for the Italians. I was shocked. Now the guards would discover that I was not who I pretended to be. I thought it was the end of me.

I walked over to the Italians. "Don't worry," the Italian master sergeant assured me. "I speak German. I just don't want them to know it. Talk to me in Italian gibberish, and I will say, 'si, si, si, si.' We don't want to be responsible for having you killed."

Eric aged nineteen, after the war, in a photo on a document identifying him as having been subjected to forced labor

I got sick and collapsed one day at the end of March in 1945. Once again, those Italians saved my life. They carried me into an abandoned mineshaft, where they had a hiding place. They fed me, and by the time the Americans came on April 16 to liberate the camp, I was on my feet again.

In 1946, if you had asked me if I was a German, I would have punched you in the nose. I could not stand Germany after what had happened. I hated every German. I wondered why I survived when others did not. I couldn't understand it. I felt I should do something about it.

I got my master's degree in engineering from a German university, and I left a week later for Israel to fight in the War of Independence. My father turned pale when I told him. He protested, "My God, you just survived the Holocaust, and now you want to get killed in another war?"

"Dad, I have to," I told him.

My graduating class sent me off with the German equivalent of "For He's a Jolly Good Fellow." It softened me a bit. I realized that not all Germans are bad. In the Israeli army, I became a human being again.

I immigrated to the United States in 1954 with my wife and five-month-old daughter. I had designed the first German car seat for babies. I brought it to my interview at the American consulate in Hamburg. The guy who interviewed me was impressed. "You designed that? It's fantastic! We want people like you to come to the United States."

In New York I worked as an engineer. It took a conscious effort to blend in. My Jewishness came from my identity as an Israeli. I was willing to talk about the War of Independence. I never wanted to talk about the Holocaust.

We settled in Pittsburgh, where we became involved in the local Jewish community. At a dinner for the Jewish Federation in Pittsburgh, the lady sitting next to me happened to be the director of Pittsburgh's Holocaust museum. She asked me, "Why don't you tell others about your experience?" A few weeks later, I called her and said, "Yes, I'll do it." I have been a Holocaust speaker ever since. It's my duty.

If anything from the Holocaust remains in me, it is that I play my part as a positive and active Jew. My daughter is married to a rabbi. My son lives in Israel. I am lucky. The Holocaust didn't touch me as much as other survivors. My experience was on a level tolerable to a human being. I was never starving. The Nazis didn't shoot my parents. I never lost contact with normal humanity.

My kids have my memoirs. Bored on airplanes on business trips overseas, I wrote my life story from thirty-five thousand feet in the air—all of it in capital letters. I had the good fortune to live an ordinary life after the war, full of ordinary pleasures. I want to make sure that other people have that same opportunity to live decent lives.

ERIC'S LESSON:
Play Your Part

Eric saw and lived through terrifying things, from the burning of his synagogue on Kristallnacht to the realities of a concentration camp. But he not only survived; he retained his dignity and his humanity. He did so through fortitude and resolve. He had the looks of a movie star and an actor's capacity to play a part, whether impersonating a member of the Hitler Youth or an Italian prisoner of war. But Eric also relied on the kindness of strangers, from the Communists who let him hide in their house to the Italians who saved him in Buchenwald. Eric took that lesson to heart. From his service in the Israeli army to his work as a Holocaust educator, he has dedicated himself to others, to ensure that no one else need endure the trauma that he did.

BIRTH: *January 26, 1939*
HOMETOWN: *Mainz, Germany*
HOLOCAUST EXPERIENCE: *Kindertransport*
LIBERATION DATE: *N/A*
IMMIGRATION TO AMERICA: *September 1943*

ERNIE HEIMANN

Treat Others as You'd Like to Be Treated

My father considered himself a German, but he also was Jewish and he was proud of it. When World War I broke out, he volunteered for the German army and was assigned to an infantry battalion on the front lines. He fought in the trenches and was awarded the Iron Cross, one of Germany's highest honors.

As the Nazis came to power, he maintained that nothing was going to happen to us because he had the Iron Cross. "My fellow veterans respect it. They wouldn't allow anything to happen to someone with an Iron Cross," he claimed.

Everything came to a head on Kristallnacht. My father had been traveling through Germany. He was trying to get home, but his friends advised him not to travel because of what was happening. He decided to stay overnight and return home the next day.

He returned a broken man. He had seen what had happened to fellow Jewish veterans with their Iron Crosses. They'd been dragged from their homes, made to clean the gutters, and then shipped off to concentration camps.

Fortunately, nothing happened to our residence during Kristallnacht. But I had been on my way to a Jewish parochial school attached to our synagogue, which was just down our street. The street, normally empty, was full of people, so I ran to see what was happening. "Don't you know? The synagogue is on fire," people said.

Devastated, I ran back to my mom. She quickly put on her coat, and we went to the synagogue. The synagogue and the school were both in flames. The firemen were there. They had their hoses ready, but they were only interested in preventing the flames from attacking neighboring property. They were content to let the synagogue burn.

With that image in our minds, we rushed home, closed the doors, and drew the blinds. From that point on, my father told us that there was no future for any Jew in Germany.

Thanks to an aunt in England, I was able to leave Germany in 1939, prior to the outbreak of World War II. I traveled in a Kindertransport. I was taken to the train station in Mainz with a suitcase. My parents put a numbered tag around my neck and promised to meet me as soon as they got permission to travel. I went to the window of the train and waved goodbye.

Then I went by ferry to England. I spent about six months in London. My parents received permission to travel to England on September 9, 1939. They had everything packed and their tickets in hand, but on September 1, World War II broke out, and the door slammed shut.

My parents tried the United States next. They had everything packed, again with their tickets in hand. The ship was to leave from Portugal on December 15, 1941. But on December 7, Pearl Harbor was attacked. That door shut too. My mother and father were locked in Germany.

My parents were put on a train to Poland. They became part of the "Final Solution." We don't know whether they succumbed to the diseases rampant in the ghetto or if they were taken to one of the killing centers.

When World War II began, I was evacuated with other London schoolchildren. We were taken to the train station and sent to Northampton, a shoe manufacturing town in the Midlands. We were told to get off the train and go with our teacher. My teacher knocked on the door of the first house on Agnes Road and said, "Mrs. Smith, the London kids are here," and pushed two of the kids into that house.

What Was the Kindertransport?

Kindertransport (German for "Children's Transport") was the informal name for rescue efforts that brought thousands of Jewish children to Britain as refugees between 1939 and 1940. The children were placed in British foster homes, hostels, schools, and farms. In many cases, they were the only members of their family to survive the Holocaust.

I ended up at 12 Agnes Road, where Mrs. Swallow opened the door. I was pushed into her home along with two other Jewish kids. Mrs. Swallow was the wife of a worker in one of the shoe factories. She had children of her own who were older and serving in the military, so she had room for us. I spent four years with Mrs. Swallow and her family.

The local kids would go to school from early morning to midday. The London kids would go from midday to late afternoon. The English took down the road signs because they were concerned about a German invasion. They put telephone poles in the flat areas so that if gliders attempted to land, their wings would get clipped.

In England, I was considered an "enemy alien." The English adults were concerned that there were German spies hiding among us. The kids, however, accepted us like locals. We were invited to join their Boy Scouts and their activities.

There was a shortage of communication supplies for the English defense force, so they recruited Boy Scouts to be messengers between various units. There I was—an enemy alien, but also a Boy Scout entrusted to run messages in case of an invasion.

We Jewish kids were fully integrated. We spent our free time with the local kids on the weekends

Ernie in 1939, aged ten

doing ordinary activities. That was one of the wonderful parts of living in Northampton.

The other wonderful thing was Mrs. Swallow herself. Hers was a working-class family; she had never met a Jew before. She was interested in learning about our religion. She tried to meet most of our dietary requirements, which was sometimes difficult. She insisted that we go to religious school and attend weekly Saturday services. She also insisted that I have a bar mitzvah. I didn't know what that was, but I had my bar mitzvah in London with my aunt. It opened my eyes to see that people like Mrs. Swallow existed.

In 1943, I was advised that my visa to go to the United States had been approved. My brother had immigrated to the United States in 1937 to continue his education; when the Japanese attacked Pearl Harbor and the United States joined the war, he volunteered for the US Army Corps. Because he was a soldier, he received permission to bring me to the United States.

My aunt took me to the train station in London and put me on a train for Liverpool. Volunteers met me at the station in Liverpool and escorted me to a ship bound for New York. I was the only kid on the ship. As a matter of fact, I was the only civilian on the ship. There were about a hundred British seamen on board whose ships had been torpedoed. They were going to the United States to get another ship to bring much-needed supplies to England.

When the seamen found out that I was traveling alone, they said, "Hey, kid, you'll be our mascot. You stick with us, and we'll take care of you. We've been torpedoed before, so we know what to do."

Three days out from land, all heck broke loose. A group of German U-boats attacked our convoy and sunk more than half its ships. Fortunately, my ship escaped the torpedoes. We were diverted north to Iceland and Greenland, where the ships could be provided with air cover. So instead of landing in New York, I landed in Halifax, Nova Scotia. I was fourteen years old and a geography buff, but I had never heard of Halifax.

Volunteers met us in Montreal and put us on a train to New York. I ended up in the arms of the aunt who was supposed to meet me. She took me to her apartment and fed me. For dessert, she prepared a banana split with whipped cream and a cherry. It was the first non-rationed meal I'd had since the Kindertransport. She put me on an overnight train to Chicago, where my uncle met me and took me to his home.

In June 1946, after I graduated high school, I wanted to enlist in the US Army to get to Germany and find out what had happened to my parents. I went to the enlisting station, and the recruiters laughed at me. "Kid, don't you know we're discharging everybody? We're not enlisting anybody. Go get a job. Go to school."

I was accepted at the Illinois Institute of Technology. I graduated, got a job, and got married in September of 1950. We started to make a life together, and then the Korean War broke out. I served two years in the army.

I didn't tell my story for years. I didn't think it was significant. When I came to the United States, everybody was looking toward the future. My focus was on making a new life for myself. But when my grandchildren were in grade school, they learned about the Holocaust in class. They had to write a paper about it, so they asked my children about my experiences.

"Grandpa never talked to us about it," my children said. "If you want to find out something, ask Grandpa." That's when I opened up and told my grandchildren my story.

The bottom line is this: Do unto others as you would like them to do unto you. That sums up everything, from bullying to how to treat immigrants. We need to remember the past, so we don't make the same mistakes again. Simple as that.

ERNIE'S LESSON:
Treat Others as You'd Like to Be Treated

Ernie says, "Do unto others as you would like them to do unto you." In England, some adults considered him an enemy, but the kids accepted him, and he was warmly welcomed into Mrs. Swallow's home. He admired Mrs. Swallow's open-mindedness and generosity. Similarly, when he was traveling to New York, the British sailors on his ship took him under their wing. Ernie's story reminds us to respect others and to value humanity.

BIRTH: *December 29, 1929*
HOMETOWN: *Frankfurt, Germany*
HOLOCAUST EXPERIENCE: *Kristallnacht; refugee from Nazi Germany*
LIBERATION DATE: *N/A*
IMMIGRATION TO AMERICA: *February 1940*
DEATH: *October 28, 2023*

FRANK STERN
Learn from the Past

I was never in a concentration camp or a ghetto. I was born in Frankfurt, Germany, in 1929. I was three years old when the Nazis came to power. My father traveled much of the year. He owned a company that distributed linings for men's suits. My mother would go to the office, and Betty, a non-Jewish woman, took care of me. She had to leave after the Nuremberg Laws were passed, so my parents combined the apartment and the office into one large apartment on Main Street.

In 1936, I started going to a Jewish school. There were only two schools like that in Frankfurt. I'd walk to the streetcar and pick up my friend Teddy on the way. We took one streetcar, transferred to another, and then walked the rest of the way. I only went to school and home. I played with the four non-Jewish boys who lived in the apartment below us. One of them belonged to the Young Folk, which was an organization for children before they became old enough to join the Hitler Youth. This boy used to play with me, go to the meetings, and come back again and play. He knew I was a Jew, but whatever indoctrination he absorbed, I wasn't a part of it.

On the last Thursday in October of 1938, the assistant principal came into my third-grade classroom and told all the Jewish students with Polish passports to go home. They were being expelled from Germany.

Even more changed before my ninth birthday. The Nazis didn't come to our apartment on Kristallnacht because we were the only Jews in our building, which wasn't in a residential area. The next morning, I went to school as usual. From the streetcar, Teddy and I saw fire engines around the main synagogue. We wanted to get off the streetcar, but we didn't. When we arrived at school, the custodian told us to go back home. There would be no school.

When I got home, my mother told me to do my homework. Just after I started it, the doorbell began ringing incessantly. Two Gestapo officers burst in. They'd come

What Were the Nuremberg Laws?

The Nuremberg Laws, passed by the Nazis in September 1935, took away Jews' basic rights. They defined Jews as a separate race from the Germans, who were called Aryans. Jews lost their German citizenship, meaning they could no longer vote in elections or hold certain jobs. Jews were also not allowed to marry non-Jewish Germans.

to arrest my father and my older brother, who was eighteen. My father was sick in bed with pneumonia. Some members of the Gestapo still had a begrudging civility, so instead of arresting my father, they told him to get a medical certificate at Gestapo headquarters. Otherwise, they threatened, they would come back.

What Was the Hitler Youth?

The Hitler Youth, formed in 1922, was the youth organization of the Nazi Party in Germany. All German boys between the ages of fourteen and eighteen were encouraged to join. The German Young Folk in the Hitler Youth, launched in 1928, was a separate group for German boys between the ages of ten and fourteen.

My brother, who was really my half brother, had been born in Switzerland. The Gestapo agents couldn't touch a foreign national. He showed them a Swiss passport, and that ended that. They ripped our phone out of the wall and stomped out.

I went back to school about two months later. For the first time in my life, I had a female teacher. Because ours was a parochial school, boys were taught by men and girls by women; the boys were in one building, the girls in another. But all the male Jewish teachers had been arrested.

After several weeks, my teacher, Mr. Marks, returned. He had been released from Dachau. His head was shaved. He said he had received an immigration visa and had come to say goodbye.

A month later, I caught diphtheria, a serious disease, and I was hospitalized. While I was there, my parents obtained a visitors' visa to Switzerland through my brother's Swiss family. I never went home again. I went directly from the hospital to Switzerland by train. We were in Lucerne for three months before my parents and I went to England. My brother stayed in Switzerland.

Frank as a young boy

In London, we went to Bow Street to get "alien" registration cards. My mother found us a single furnished room in a rooming house. By that point, I hadn't attended school for a year. My mother found a school about three hours away from London by train. War was imminent. The English were distributing gas masks. My gas mask and I went off on a train to school. I was in school for several weeks before the war broke out. Bombs started falling around us. Our school was on the coast, so the English authorities moved us inland to a safer place.

By the time I got back to London for winter vacation, I was pretty fluent in English. The bombings hadn't yet started, but school did not return to session. People were being evacuated from London.

My father had applied for a visa to the United States in 1935. Our number came up in 1940. We went to Liverpool on the west coast of England and then took a British merchant ship to the United States. I was ten. My mother made packets for us to wear around our neck with our papers in case our boat was sunk. Without papers, you were nobody.

The ship was crowded. We were stuffed in a corridor and slept on the floor with other refugees—including a physician who later became our doctor in New York.

When we arrived in the United States, we stayed in New York first, then moved to Louisville, Kentucky, where my aunt lived.

There, I started going to school again. It was strange enough having girls in the class, but it never occurred to me that there were no Black students. I didn't realize the school was segregated until my family was preparing to move back to New York. One of the girls asked me, "What happens if you have to sit next to a colored girl in New York?" I looked at her as if she were crazy, and I said, "So what?"

I never considered myself a survivor. I always thought survivors had been in concentration camps or ghettos. But I now understand that we were all survivors. I share my story often, discussing the importance of learning from the past. We need to remember that history is not one-size-fits-all. But there are patterns, and we need to recognize them.

FRANK'S LESSON:
Learn from the Past

Frank started speaking about the Holocaust for the forty-eighth anniversary of Kristallnacht. He sees his story as a warning. He wants future generations to learn from his experience so that other children do not suffer the isolation, loneliness, and dislocation of being a refugee. Frank's story invites us to learn from the past to face the future. History gives us a perspective that can guide us through the challenges that come our way.

BIRTH: *February 1, 1933*
HOMETOWN: *Montabaur, Germany*
HOLOCAUST EXPERIENCE:
Concentration camp survivor
LIBERATION DATE: *May 1945*
IMMIGRATION TO AMERICA: *1949*
DEATH: *September 1, 2020*

JUDY STRAUS
Fight for Your Rights

I was born in Montabaur, Germany, in 1933. I'm an only child. My mother stayed at home, cooking, cleaning, and playing bridge, as many mothers did. My father worked as an electrical engineer. He was immediately fired when Hitler came to power. My father knew he wouldn't find work in Germany, so my parents moved to Amsterdam in Holland (the Netherlands) soon after I was born. Holland had been a neutral country during World War I. I stayed with my grandparents in Germany until I was about a year old and then joined my parents in Holland.

Until I was seven, life was pretty good. My father started a successful business. I had friends in school. Then, in May of 1940, the Germans invaded Holland, and things started to change.

We tried to escape in a ship across the English Channel, but only fishing boats were available. No one had the nerve to escape in one of those, so we returned to Amsterdam.

One by one, laws were implemented that took away all our privacy and pleasure. We weren't allowed to go to public school. We had to go to Jewish schools. We couldn't go to the movies. We moved into a ghetto. There, I was introduced to fleas. I remember my father coming home and getting in the bathtub because, if you soaked underwater, the fleas would die.

The Germans started rounding up Jewish people and sending them to concentration camps. Not everybody reported voluntarily, so the Germans started raiding the neighborhood after our 8 p.m. curfew, when we had to be in our apartments.

Every day, on the way home from school, I was afraid that my parents would not be in the apartment when I returned, that they had been picked up by the Germans.

We were able to stay in our Amsterdam apartment in the ghetto until 1943. My father was teaching in the Jewish school, so he was exempt from transport to the concentration camps. Then, on my mother's fortieth birthday, the Germans closed the ghetto. Everybody prepared to go to a transit camp called Westerbork.

What Was Westerbork?

Located in the northeastern part of the Netherlands, Westerbork served as a transit camp, a temporary stop for Dutch Jews before they were deported to killing centers. Canadian forces liberated Westerbork on April 12, 1945.

Every Monday, a train came into Westerbork with railcars filled with people. The barracks at Westerbork were huge. The men slept on one side and the women and children on the other.

About two thousand Jewish prisoners were in charge of the everyday operations of the camp. They served as a police force. They would come into the barracks and read the names of those who were being sent from Westerbork to a concentration camp. Each time a name was called, it was awful. Some people were quiet, but many were upset. I will never forget the sounds. It was pure horror. After a transport, the barracks were much emptier.

In Westerbork, the trick was to stay off the train. If you were on the train, you knew you were going to Auschwitz or Bergen-Belsen. It was considered a privilege to go to Bergen-Belsen; Auschwitz meant certain death.

Our turn came on September 4, 1944. The train ride was horrible. It was very crowded. There was no toilet, no water, and no food. The men took turns looking through a little crack in the wood to try to see where we were going.

I think I must have fainted because I don't remember much. I remember eating porridge that my mother had made for me. But I remember nothing else.

After two days, we arrived at Theresienstadt in Czechoslovakia. We were

What Was Bergen-Belsen?

Located in northern Germany, Bergen-Belsen was transformed from a prisoner-exchange camp into a concentration camp in March 1944. Poor sanitary conditions, epidemics, and starvation led to the deaths of thousands, including Anne Frank and her sister, Margot, who died there shortly before the camp was liberated on April 15, 1945.

What Was Theresienstadt?

Theresienstadt is the German name for the Czech town of Terezín, located about 40 miles (64 km) from Prague. It was a camp in which many children, artists, and musicians were imprisoned. Nazis used the Theresienstadt ghetto, established in November 1941, as a "model Jewish settlement" to show Red Cross investigators how well Jews were being treated. In reality, thousands died from starvation and disease, and thousands more were deported to killing centers. Over fifteen thousand children died in Theresienstadt.

welcomed by terrifying barking dogs and shouting Nazis who told us to leave all our luggage on the train, that it would be delivered to us later. We weren't allowed to take anything with us. But there was one book that I loved, *The Seasons*. On the inside, I had written, *This book belongs to Ulla*—that's what people called me. I grabbed the book, and I still have it to this day.

We had to take off our clothes. The guards said we would be disinfected, but we didn't believe that. We knew about the gas chambers. We all sat there, waiting to be killed.

Then the guards sent my father to one barracks and my mother and me to another. Theresienstadt was built in the middle of the 1800s to house nine thousand soldiers. When we arrived, there were fifty thousand people there.

My father wasn't put to work. We couldn't figure out why. However, my mother was sent to a quarry to split mica, a kind of mineral. She had to fulfill a daily quota. I still have some of the mica she dug out in those years. I worked as a messenger between the offices of the camp.

Then the Nazis sent my father and other men from our Dutch transport to work camps across Europe. I remember walking with my father to the train that would take him away. He told me not to tell my mother; she was already so worried.

I had been sick in Westerbork. I was sick in Theresienstadt. I got headaches. My legs were wobbly. I had trouble getting into my bunk. I was dizzy all the time. My mother was working sixteen hours a day, but she finally found a doctor. His name was Dr. Korob, and he said to me, "Bring your finger to your nose." I couldn't do it, so he said, "You have encephalitis. You're contagious."

I ended up in a barracks for contagious people. The sheets were filthy and I wanted to get out of there. I finally convinced them that I was not contagious.

My mother was worried that I had nobody to watch over me while she was at work, so she put me into an orphanage. I was not happy and I wanted to tell her, but I didn't. She already had it tough enough.

There was a swing at the orphanage. The kids who weren't in the orphanage weren't allowed to use it, so I got to swing while other children watched. One day all those other children were transferred to another camp. They were gone. I had felt good being on the swing, but as time went on, I started feeling bad about it. I felt guilty that I was okay, and the other kids might not have been. It still affects how I look at children on swings today.

We were liberated in 1945 by Soviet troops. The camp was in the middle of a typhoid epidemic. The Soviets didn't want us to leave the camp until the epidemic was under control, so we remained in Theresienstadt for a month. Once we were allowed to leave, we were just given a ride in a truck to the station. Then we waited until a train arrived. It took many days to get back to Amsterdam.

When I returned, I decided I wasn't going to talk or think about the camp. I avoided kids who I knew had been in a camp. The other kids who had been there avoided me too. Nobody wanted to talk about Theresienstadt. Even the adults didn't talk to one another about their experiences at first. It was a taboo subject.

My uncle had been in hiding for two years and, unlike my father, survived. He took on the father role and guided me to high school. I liked high school. I was living the life of a normal twelve-year-old. We had all kinds of activities, including dance lessons. I was on the hockey team. Nobody asked me what had happened during the war.

We came to America in 1949. I had a rough time because I wanted to look and act like the American kids. My name was Ursel, but on the boat, we were told that we could change our names before we registered at the entry port. I asked my American uncle what the most popular name in America was and he said, "Judy." That became my American name.

My school didn't offer English as a second language. You had to learn the curriculum the way it was. I didn't get my usual high grades. I even flunked chemistry. The girls at school were nice, though. They would invite me for lunch. It took me two years to feel comfortable with life in America.

Judy as a young woman

When I was twenty-two, I fell in love and got married. We had three kids and a nice family life. My kids knew that I'd been in the concentration camps. They must have understood how it affected me, so they never asked about it.

I started talking about my Holocaust experiences when I was sixty-six. In the beginning, I could talk about it with a group of students—but not at home. Now, my own children ask me about my experience, and my oldest went on a trip to Theresienstadt to learn our family's history.

JUDY'S LESSON:
Fight for Your Rights

Judy's story conveys the importance of protecting our human and civil rights. One way to do so is by voting in elections. "Our voter turnout is abysmal compared to some other countries," Judy says of the United States. "It's important that everybody votes. I'm not able to ring as many doorbells as I used to, but I still make phone calls." Judy works to protect the rights of the vulnerable. Although she waited many years to speak publicly about the Holocaust, she now believes it's important to share her story. She used to tell the children that experiences like hers couldn't happen in America, but low voter turnout makes her worry, since citizens need to participate in their democracy for it to work.

BIRTH: *June 11, 1927*
HOMETOWN: *Miskolc, Hungary*
HOLOCAUST EXPERIENCE:
Concentration camp survivor
LIBERATION DATE: *March 1945*
IMMIGRATION TO AMERICA:
September 1946
DEATH: *July 7, 2020*

MAGDA BROWN
Never Again

At age fourteen, I graduated from middle school. Only 1 percent of Jewish children were admitted into higher education. My grades were good, and my father could afford tuition, but I didn't make that 1 percent. That was my first experience of discrimination.

As I wrestled with this personal disappointment, the Nazis arrived in Hungary. It was March 1944.

In no time, we received orders to wear a yellow star sewn onto our clothing. Without it, we were not permitted to go out. Even children who had no idea what the Star of David meant had to wear it. In

April, all Jewish people in the countryside and the suburban areas were ordered to move into a ghetto.

Miskolc, where I lived, was a big city. My house, which my grandfather had built forty years earlier, became part of the ghetto. Six people lived in that house: my parents, my aunt and uncle, my brother, and me.

When the police escorts brought people in from the outlying areas, they wouldn't look inside the houses to see how much space there was. They shoved people into our home, which became the residence of forty people. You cannot fathom what problems such crowded conditions can cause. These people were totally exhausted because they had traveled to the city on foot, each with a little overnight case. Every human behavior was visible in my house: there was the silent one, the crying one, the cursing one, the praying one. Each new arrival had to find a little corner in this crowded house to lay their tired body down.

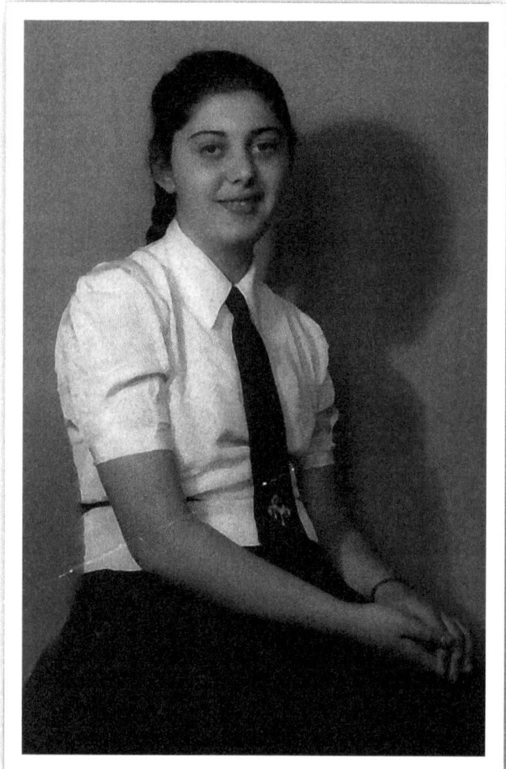

Magda in her school uniform

Once we were incarcerated in the ghetto, we were no longer free to roam in public. No school, no business, no employment of any sort was permitted. However, life in the ghetto didn't last long. At the beginning of June, the Nazis told us that we each had to pack a bag and that we'd be taken to another country where they needed laborers.

Who questions something like that? We thought, "It's wartime. The Germans need laborers, so we'll go and do our work. When the war is over, we'll come home, and life will continue." Unfortunately, it didn't work out that way. It was only a ploy to keep us calm.

We had to march across the city to a brickyard. It had no housing, no bathrooms, and no water—nothing but bricks. We couldn't figure out why the Germans would bring us there. But the Holocaust was premeditated, systematically coordinated mass murder. They took us to the brickyard, we learned, because the brickyard was adjacent to the railroad tracks.

On June 11, 1944, my seventeenth birthday, the Nazis began loading us into railcars. I was forced into a car with about seventy-five other people. There was enough space for thirty. It was so crowded that I stood for three consecutive days, shifting this way and that way to allow my parents to sit on the wooden floor.

There were two buckets in the boxcar: one to use as a toilet, the other to wash ourselves. But the wash bucket wasn't refilled. The most painful feeling was thirst. It was worse than any physical pain.

On the second day, the train crossed the Carpathian Mountains, which separate Hungary from Czechoslovakia. I was pushed up against a little window not bigger than a laptop. I looked out and saw beautiful countryside: lush green grass and trees. In the distance, I spotted a shepherd minding his flock. "Why is he out there and I am in here?" I asked myself.

On the third day, we arrived in Auschwitz-Birkenau. I had absolutely no idea that such a place existed. Guards in uniform boarded the train. "Leave your baggage here. You will get it later," they told us. "Later" never came. Our last mementos from home were gone forever.

We exited the train and lined up: women and children in one row, men in another. The men's group marched off. That was the last time I saw my father. Then came the sorting. We stood in front of five Nazi officers. One of them was Dr. Mengele.

To the Nazis, we were not human beings anymore. They would just point to select us. My mother, who was a young-looking forty-two-year-old, was holding onto me. Mengele pointed at me. I turned to my mother and said, "I'll see you later, Mother," but I never saw her again.

Those who weren't murdered were led into a big, empty room with a wooden floor. "Fold up your clothes, lay them down, and remember where you put them," the guards ordered us. They shaved our heads and all our body hair. In the next room, we saw bald-headed girls and heard them scream as the Nazis sprayed disinfectant on their freshly shaven skin.

We were bald too. We looked into each other's eyes and listened to each other's voices until, eventually, we recognized one another. From there, we went into "the shower," which was a big room with fifty showerheads screwed into the ceiling. There was no soap, no towel—just cold water that trickled down on your dirty, smelly body.

In the next room was a mountain of clothing reaching the ceiling. There were piles and piles of clothing of different shapes and sizes. Prisoners threw garments at you: they didn't look at you to see if you were tall, short, fat, or skinny.

I ended up with a long, ill-fitting gown. The Nazis stole our shoes and gave us flip-flops—like kids wear today—but the sole was a thick piece of wood with a leather strap to hold the shoe on your foot. They were difficult to walk in. To this day, I have a scar between my ankle and my foot where the leather band rubbed off my skin and it became infected. There was no medication for prisoners in Auschwitz.

Five hundred people slept in a barracks made for three hundred. To make us fit, there were five rows of a hundred people lying sideways, like sardines in a can. Our shoes were our pillows. The body next to us was our blanket.

Every day we were sorted. One group was told to go this way, and one group somewhere else. We were in the camp for four days before we started asking the old-timers, "Could you please tell us how soon we're going to meet the people who went the other way?" The old-timers pointed to the five chimneys of the crematorium.

We saw heavy black smoke spewing out of the chimneys, and there was a burning odor. We had no idea that something like the crematorium existed. This is the twentieth century, we thought. People die of natural causes or illnesses. No one is murdered because of hatred and discrimination. Surely, we thought, the Germans couldn't be so barbaric as to put people in gas chambers. We were in a state of shock.

I was seventeen years old and all alone. But even in unbelievable conditions, you can still find mentors. There were three sisters from my city, who were a couple of years older than me. They cared for me. Once, they found me crying on the bunk. "What's the matter with you?" one of the sisters asked.

"I am so hungry I can't see straight," I said. The sisters always had saved a crust of bread in case we didn't get fed in the morning, and they pooled their crusts of bread to share with me. That was the most beautiful gesture in the world.

From morning, when we left the room, until evening when it was time to sleep, we were not permitted to be in the shade. The yards in Auschwitz were gravel: no trees, no grass. Hiding from the sun was a challenge.

"Did you give up faith in God in Auschwitz?" people ask me. But when you grow up in a religious household, as I did, you don't consider giving up your faith. There were some religious women, a bit older than us. I don't know how they knew when Shabbat was, but somehow, they knew. The only place we could be uninterrupted was behind the latrines, and the women would pull us back there to pray.

Every day, the guards lined us up and sorted us for work. One day, a unit of a thousand Hungarian women, including me, was selected. I had been in Auschwitz for two months. The Nazis put us into a railcar and shipped us to Germany, to an ammunition factory near the city of Marburg. We were just kids. We had never seen a factory, let alone worked in one, but you'd be surprised how fast you learn when you must.

We worked twelve-hour shifts. I worked the daytime shift, so I never saw sunlight. I was working with highly poisonous material without any protective garments. The poisons started invading my body. My face became lemon yellow, and my lips were deep, dark purple.

At the end of March 1945, the Nazis suddenly evacuated the camp and forced us on a "death march." We didn't know where we were going. We walked many miles without food. Our legs were bare. It was bitterly cold. All day, we walked on the highway. At night, we slept on the wet ground in ditches. When you're exhausted, you can fall asleep anywhere.

At the end of the fourth day of marching, we were standing before a big field. On the far side of the field, we spotted a barn, about two city blocks away. We started to fantasize that maybe during the night, we could crawl on our stomachs and reach that barn and hide. If the guards found us, they'd shoot us. But we were desperate, so we tried it—and we made it successfully to the barn.

The next morning, we looked out a peephole from the barn and saw two young men walking toward us. We were scared. We didn't know who they were. They turned out to be two scouts from the Sixth Armored Division of the US Army. They were our liberators!

MAGDA'S LESSON:
Never Again

Magda believes that to stop genocide, we must eliminate hatred. In October 2018, following the shooting at the Tree of Life synagogue in Pittsburgh, Magda was asked if she wished to cancel a scheduled speaking engagement. "No," she said. "They need to hear my story now more than ever." Magda's commitment and bravery show that we must work to eliminate hatred through basic gestures of love and courage.

BIRTH: *April 26, 1936*
HOMETOWN: *Amsterdam, the Netherlands*
HOLOCAUST EXPERIENCE:
Concentration camp survivor
LIBERATION DATE: *September 12, 1944*
IMMIGRATION TO AMERICA:
April 25, 1951

RODI GLASS
Help a Stranger

I am an only child because of the war. My parents thought that if something bad was going to happen with war coming, one child would be enough. Most of my family members were murdered.

In Holland, my parents and grandparents lived much like we live here in the United States. We were comfortable before the war. We were Jewish, but we also were Dutch. Nobody called us "dirty Jews." The Dutch let us live freely. We had the same rights as everybody else. We could go where we pleased.

Then, in 1940, the Germans invaded the Netherlands, and in

1942, they started deporting people to concentration camps. As soon as the Nazis arrived, things changed. We weren't allowed to go to parks or to school, and we weren't allowed to be out after a certain time. We weren't allowed to ride bicycles or the streetcars. We had to wear the yellow Star of David—a way to identify and isolate Jews. There was a Dutch Nazi Party, and many people who lived in our country turned against the Jews.

On the night of September 28, 1942, my mom, my dad, and I were arrested in our home and put on a military truck that took us to the central railway station in Amsterdam. From there, we were sent to Westerbork transit camp.

The train took us to a town called Hooghalen. We had to walk the rest of the way, five or ten kilometers [3 to 6 miles], in the middle of the night. It was raining and muddy. I was six years old.

We were some of the first people to arrive in Westerbork. The barracks were still being built. My parents worked, but I didn't because I was a child. I sat and did nothing. I didn't get much food. The long barracks held 350 people. There was one toilet. There were no showers or mattresses, but there were plenty of lice.

From Westerbork, people were sent to concentration camps in the East. Every day, the Nazis counted the prisoners. One day, my mother recognized one of the Nazi guards. He had lived on our street. He used to hang out at my grandmother's house. He and my mother had been good friends. Maybe he thought that becoming a Nazi would help him, or that it would make him seem smarter or more important. Whatever his reason, he became one of them.

My mother looked at him; he looked at my mother. With his eyes, he said, "Don't say hello. Don't show you recognize me." He had a list with the names of all the prisoners; he removed our names. Had he

Rodi at about aged four

not done that, we would have been on one of the first transports to Auschwitz.

While we were in Westerbork, my parents tried to get a form from the German government that said that, at least for a while, we couldn't be shipped east. "A while" could be in the next hour or the next day. It could be anytime the Nazis decided. At that time, nobody except the Germans knew that east meant death.

The form came through, and we were released from the camp. We returned home. A year later, in 1943, a German soldier confiscated our family business. He knew nothing about the business, so he kept my mother on to help him. She put aside the money that she earned to feed us.

By September 1943, there weren't many Jews left in Holland. We noticed that people were disappearing and being sent to the concentration camps. There was no time to say goodbye. There was no phone communication. You only saw one another on the street and in each other's homes. Then the Nazis rounded up all the remaining Jews in Amsterdam, forcing us from our homes into a ghetto. We got a notice to go to the train station, and we were put on the last transport from Amsterdam to Westerbork.

I was fortunate that my mom was born in England. When we arrived at Westerbork this time, we heard that if you were born in America or England, you were to go to a different camp. So, in early 1943, my family was sent to the Vittel internment camp in France.

Vittel had been a spa. Spas have hotels; the Germans needed rooms. There was no land at the spa to build barracks, but they put up barbed wire to imprison Jews as well as non-Jews who were British subjects or American citizens. That's where I spent the rest of the war, until we were liberated.

Holland remained occupied until 1945, so we couldn't go home right away. We had no money, no clothes. I had no education. I had no childhood. Our lives were the most valuable thing we had. I was nine when I left the camps. I knew nothing except how to read.

After Holland was liberated, my mother got papers from the consulate in Paris, and we returned to Amsterdam on a train. The journey lasted three days and three nights, and we had no food or water. We arrived in Amsterdam in June 1945. When we got off the train, the authorities gave us each a lanyard, a sign that said *Homeless*, and ten guilders. We stayed in an orphanage.

Our family store was still there, and the Nazi was still there. My father threw him out. The police didn't care. There was no merchandise to sell.

My father started a school for the children who had been in the camps or in hiding. All ages were educated together, as we all had to learn from the ground up. Once we had caught up, we went to regular schools, and life took on some normalcy.

What Was Vittel?

Vittel was originally a resort in northeastern France, near the German border. The Nazis turned it into an internment camp in 1941. It primarily held citizens of enemy countries residing in France. Most of Vittel's Jewish detainees were deported to Auschwitz-Birkenau and murdered. The camp was liberated by the US Army on September 12, 1944.

When we returned to Amsterdam, people said hurtful things. "Oh, you came back? So the Nazis only killed the good ones." Or they'd say to my father, "How come you came back and your twin brother didn't? He was the nice one."

Before the war, my mother had beautiful table linens and silverware and clothes, which she had given to a Christian neighbor to hide for us. After we returned, she went to the neighbor. My mother had nothing but the clothes she was wearing. She rang the doorbell. When our neighbor answered the door, she was wearing my mother's dress. "Hello," my mother said. "Do you remember me? Do you still have my things?"

The woman looked at her and said, "I don't know who you are," and slammed the door. People weren't happy to see us come back. They wanted to keep our possessions, our homes, and our businesses.

My aunts were already in America. They urged us to join them. My parents and I came to the United States the day after I turned fifteen. We didn't come as refugees; 1951 was peacetime, so we were considered immigrants.

We came to Chicago, where my aunts lived. I had to start my life again. I had to adjust to a new environment, speak a different language, and learn a different culture. I went to high school and learned English. People were not used to foreigners. They looked at me like I was a strange bird, so I spent a lot of time with my family. I didn't have a lot of friends. After high school, I became a party planner because I like parties and I like to be happy.

For many years after my family and others returned from the camps, nobody spoke about the Holocaust. When we came to America, most Americans didn't understand what had happened to us. Nobody cared. Nobody wanted to hear our stories. One woman told my grandfather, "You think it was so easy in the United States? We couldn't get silk stockings." After that, my grandfather said we would never talk about the Holocaust outside the house again. We only spoke about it among ourselves.

Most people in America never knew I was a Holocaust survivor. I never planned to tell my story. I was busy. I had a life, a business, three children to raise. Then, one day, I met someone I knew from high school who encouraged me to speak about my experiences. Speaking about the Holocaust has become a big part of my life.

Young people today are witnessing the last living Holocaust survivors. We're not going to be around much longer. I feel an obligation to tell my story so nobody can deny that the Holocaust happened. It did happen.

RODI'S LESSON:
Help a Stranger

Rodi's story shows what can happen when neighbor turns against neighbor, but it also shows the power of helping strangers. In becoming a Holocaust speaker, Rodi dedicated herself to helping people, including others who have had experiences similar to hers. "People from Rwanda and Sudan, countries with genocides—I relate to them," she says. By telling her story, she hopes to help strangers, ensuring they don't suffer in silence the way she and her family did.

BIRTH: *February 13, 1930*
HOMETOWN: *Berlin, Germany*
HOLOCAUST EXPERIENCE: *Refugee from Nazi Germany*
LIBERATION DATE: *N/A*
IMMIGRATION TO AMERICA: *August 1941*

RUTH STERN

Adapt to Survive

I was born in 1930 in Berlin. My father was a dentist. My mother was a typist. We lived in an apartment with a balcony, on one of the main streets of Berlin.

In 1933, when Hitler came to power, there were big marches staged like Hollywood movies. I was enthusiastic about Hitler because of the parades. I stood on the balcony and watched. It felt like the parade was designed for my entertainment. My parents were less entertained.

My father decided that we should leave Germany, that it was no place for Jews. We moved to Antwerp, Belgium, where he had a sister.

In Antwerp, the front of our apartment was my father's new dentist office and waiting room. It was always busy. My father trained my mother to become his attendant. She cleaned the instruments and developed the X-rays in a darkroom.

I had a happy life in Belgium. I didn't know that my father was trying to leave. After the Germans occupied the Rhineland, he got worried. "We'd better get out of the whole continent," he said.

He tried to move us to England, but the English passed a law that said foreign doctors and dentists wouldn't get working papers. He also tried Australia and New Zealand, but those countries passed the same law. At that point, he applied to the United States. But there was an immigration quota, and our number would not come up before 1942.

Who knew what was going to happen? We were packed, but we couldn't leave Belgium. We were still there on June 11, 1940. I learned what a swastika meant that day. We woke up to the noise of low-flying planes painted with swastikas, dropping bombs. "The Germans are invading," my father explained.

My mother was practical. The first thing she did was take our money out of the bank. Who knew when we would be able to go to the bank again?

Anybody who wasn't a citizen had to go to the local school and register, so my father, like a good person, went to register. Meanwhile, my mother decided it was too dangerous to stay; we were being bombed all the time. We went out to look for somebody with enough gas money to take us south.

My mother and I saw Jewish men being marched through town, many of whom we knew. They had been rounded up by the Germans. Among the marchers, my mother found my father. She went quickly to the nearest grocery store to buy fruit, and she threw apples and oranges to the men to help them on their journey. She repeated this several times, running to different grocery stores, keeping up with the marchers to provide them sustenance.

We didn't see my father again until the next year. He had been put into a railcar and sent to a camp in southern France called Saint-Cyprien. Later, my father was deported to the Gurs internment camp in southwestern France.

It was during this time that we took in a young girl who had been abandoned by her parents. Her name was also Ruth. Ruth's mother had obtained papers to go to England as a domestic servant, and her father had escaped to Switzerland. She had no one to take care of her, so Ruth became a member of our family.

Soon, my mother, Ruth, and I started walking with all the other refugees to France. My mother carried the suitcase, and we held poles with blankets containing our things. Being a careful person, my mother had put all our money and possessions into a large bag. I still remember its shape and color. She used it as a pillow.

You may have seen pictures of refugees walking on roads being bombed. We were those refugees, trying to walk faster than the Germans' advance. But the Germans advanced fast. They strafed the roads from above. We were in farm country, and we'd dive into roadside ditches and come out covered in cow manure. There was no place to wash.

What Were Saint-Cyprien and Gurs?

The Saint-Cyprien internment camp and the Gurs internment camp were lesser-known camps in France, originally set up to accommodate refugees from the Spanish Civil War (1936–1939). During World War II, the Nazis used these camps to confine Jews and political prisoners.

Ruth complained less than I did. She was more compliant. We were hungry, but we managed. The stores were all closed, or they were open but the owners said, "The refugees already ate everything edible."

My mother saw a can of peas, but she didn't have a can opener. "If I pay you, will you open the can?" she asked a passerby. "We'll eat out of the can." To this day, I love those little white Le Sueur peas. We drank their juice because we were thirsty. Some people would give you water, but none of the locals could spend the whole day standing around giving out water.

The three of us went some distance by train, until the bombs destroyed the rails. We got off in a place called Poperinge. People were crying in the railroad station because they'd lost their papers. I was ten years old, and when I saw those people crying, I learned that papers are important. "Without papers, you are nobody," my mother said. "You have no rights, no nothing."

There were many dead people on the streets. That's when I saw my first dead bodies. I remember the first one. She was a pretty woman in a bright green long-sleeved dress. I can still see her. I wasn't frightened of the dead. They didn't look like monsters. They looked like people who were just lying there. It hadn't yet set in that they were dead.

We managed to find a farm. I'd never been on a farm. Other refugees were there. We slept on hay in a barn. I slept well on the hay, and for a few pennies, I could get milk right from the cow. It was still warm. I'd never had that before.

We left the farm and walked until we saw the fence of the French border. At the border, another refugee asked my mother, "What passport do you have? Are you a citizen?"

"No. I'm German," she said.

"In France, you will be interned as soon as you cross the border, and then you'll be helpless," the refugee said, so we turned around and retreated to Belgium with the others.

We stayed in shelters. We ended up in a place called De Panne, close to the water on a beach facing England. The shelter was in a dune. Thirty people slept on the sand with their things, facing each other in two rows.

It rained all night. We knew that the guns were nearby. Shrapnel came through the door, going into Ruth's mouth and past her eye. My mother used a blanket, not the most sanitary thing, to stanch the bleeding.

As soon as daylight came, my mother somehow communicated with a British soldier. She had the address of Ruth's biological mother in England. She asked the soldier to take Ruth because the Germans were coming and she was a Jew. He took her. We would have kept her until she was an adult, but my mother thought it was the right thing to do.

Eventually, the guns quieted down. Now there were two of us, my mother and me. When daylight came, we went to the beach, got rid of our bloody things, and picked up nice warm khaki blankets left by the British Army. We wrapped whatever we had in them to carry back to Antwerp. I still have one of the blankets. My kids still go camping with it.

My mother and I went to a hotel in Ostend, Belgium. The city was crowded, but my mother found a guy with a double bed. "If I put my daughter between us, can I have the other part of the bed?" she asked him. That's where we slept in Ostend.

The water had been bombed out. You can't drink seawater, so we drank beer. Belgians drink beer all the time. Germans didn't give kids beer, but Belgian kids got beer, sometimes even in a bottle. I've never liked beer since.

We made our way back to Antwerp. There, somebody approached

me as I was playing in the street. "Do you know somebody named Ruth?" this person asked me. "She wants to go back to her mother in Antwerp." That's how we eventually reunited.

We learned from Ruth that the British soldiers had taken her to a convent to recover. We were able to locate her father in Switzerland and reunite them, and she received proper medical care for her eye injury. Many years later, she would move to the United States, and again we'd be reunited. That is another story.

Ruth as a child, with her bike

My mother shipped everything she could, and we took a train to Paris. It was an unusually cold winter. Nothing was heated. The Germans had used up all the coal, but my mother found a building that was rented out to refugees. It was warm enough.

The two of us were there for six weeks. My mother found a smuggler to take us from occupied France to so-called unoccupied France—which wasn't so unoccupied. The smuggler took us on a train to Tours. In Tours, we went to a restaurant and walked through to the back. We stayed there until nighttime.

At night, we were taken to a farm. The farmer got out of bed, got dressed in front of us, and took us out walking through his fields. It must have rained because it was muddy. I heard shooting, but it didn't scare me. When we got to the other end of the fields, there was a driver who drove us the rest of the way.

My father's sister obtained a visa for my mother, my father, and me. So my father was able to get out of the camp in Gurs. A year after we were separated, I met him again at another camp near Marseille.

Getting an exit permit was hard. The Vichy authorities wouldn't give us one, so my father sat on an official's desk in desperation and said, "If you want to keep us, that's okay. You've been feeding me for the last year, and you'll have to continue feeding me and my family if you don't let me go." The official gave him the exit permit.

My parents, Ruth, and I went on the ship of a French company that took bananas from Martinique to Marseille. The company put bunks where there used to be bananas. There were three boats, and we were on the third. The British seized the first boat in Bermuda because they said there was a spy on board. The second boat got stuck in Dakar, and we got stuck in Casablanca because the company wasn't going to risk getting more of their ships caught by the British. We stayed a long time in the harbor.

Eventually, the French tired of keeping us in the harbor, so they interned us at the foot of the Atlas Mountains. I stayed overnight at a school, and then I went on a bus. We were on the top of the bus and got sunburned. Half a day later, we arrived in the Sidi-al-Ayachi internment camp, where we slept in bunks with netting and straw mattresses.

My maternal grandfather managed to get us places on a Portuguese ship that sailed between Portugal, Casablanca, and the United States. He

What Was Vichy France?

Vichy France is the common name of the French State headed by Marshal Philippe Pétain during World War II. It was an independent ally of Nazi Germany until late 1942 when Berlin took full control. Its capital was located in the city of Vichy.

had immigrated to the United States in the beginning of 1939 to be with his son, who had immigrated in 1928.

What Was Sidi-al-Ayachi?

The Sidi-al-Ayachi internment camp held Jewish refugees who arrived in Morocco without visas or papers. It also housed political prisoners. It was one of about thirty camps in Morocco during the war.

My mother and I arrived in America in August of 1941. My mother dropped me off with her parents in Chicago, where I lived for a year. I learned English. My father was stuck for a while, but eventually he made it to the United States before Pearl Harbor. Finally, we were all in the same country. We moved to St. Louis, Missouri, and then to New York.

People must adapt to survive. Whatever unexpected challenges you face along life's journey, you must stay positive and adapt to your new life.

RUTH'S LESSON:
Adapt to Survive

Ruth learned to adapt to disruptions and displacements from an early age by watching her parents make the best of each new situation. Adaptation became a way of life for Ruth. Her story reveals extraordinary resilience. She offers an example of facing challenges with dignity and grace. But her story also encourages us to learn the lessons of history: to recognize dangerous happenings early on and stop them.

GLOSSARY

antisemitism: prejudice against or hatred of Jews

bar mitzvah: a Jewish coming-of-age ritual, typically at the age of thirteen; also, bat mitzvah for girls

concentration camp: a place where large numbers of political prisoners or members of persecuted minority groups are imprisoned, sometimes to provide forced labor or to await deportation; may also be referred to as an internment camp

Czechoslovakia: a former country in central Europe that existed from 1918–1992 and included present-day Slovakia and the Czech Republic

death march: the brutal forced movement of concentration camp prisoners, often on foot, away from approaching Allied troops in early 1945

deportation: removal from a country

displaced persons: Jews and others who did not wish—or were not able—to return to their countries of origin at the end of the war and were placed in displaced person camps until they could find other places to live

"Final Solution": a term used by Nazi leaders for the plan to murder every Jewish person in occupied Europe

gas chamber: a sealed room in a concentration camp where poisonous gas was used to murder people

genocide: the deliberate, systematic destruction of a group of people based on their national, ethnic, racial, or religious identity

Gestapo: the German Secret State Police, one of the most feared entities in German-occupied areas

kapo: a Nazi concentration camp prisoner who received privileges in return for supervising other prisoners

killing centers: centers established by the Nazis solely for quick, efficient mass murder; also known as death camps or death factories

liberation: the freeing of concentration camp prisoners by Allied forces

Nazi: a member of the National Socialist German Workers' Party, formed in 1920, which promised Germans a strong central government, a national community based on race, and the racial "cleansing" of Jews

Soviet: related to the Soviet Union, a former country in eastern Europe that existed from 1922–1991 and included present-day Russia

Star of David: a six-pointed star that is a centuries-old symbol of Judaism; a star, often yellow, that Jews had to wear on badges or armbands during the Nazi regime

swastika: an ancient symbol adopted by the Nazi regime

ACKNOWLEDGMENTS

Thank you to Aaron and AJ Greenberg of Biograph LLC and to Matthew Sackel for your dedication to preserving and sharing Holocaust survivors' stories.

Thank you to the staff, board members, leadership, and volunteers of the Illinois Holocaust Museum for the work you do every day to remember the past and to transform the future.

Thank you to our incredible agent, Dan Strutzel, for finding a home for this book, and to Joni Sussman and the team at Kar-Ben for believing in the value of these stories.

Most of all, thank you to Adele, Barney, Eric, Ernie, Frank, Judy, Magda, Rodi, and Ruth for entrusting us with your stories. It is an honor to help tell them, and it is a pleasure to know you. May Adele's, Judy's, Magda's, and Frank's memories be a blessing.

ILLINOIS HOLOCAUST MUSEUM & EDUCATION CENTER

AMANDA FRIEDEMAN is a veteran educator with expertise in Holocaust, genocide, and human rights education, media literacy, and multi-disciplinary learning. She is a nationally-recognized expert on teaching with Holocaust survivor testimony and incorporating voices of the Second Generation into Holocaust education. Her work as an executive producer of three virtual reality films on the Holocaust has been awarded official selections at film festivals.

KELLEY SZANY is an internationally recognized leader in Holocaust, genocide, and museum education. She serves on the board of directors for the Association of Holocaust Organizations and Educators' Institute for Human Rights. Szany has produced ten documentary and virtual reality films on the Holocaust. She has also authored scholarly works, with recent publications in *Teaching about Genocide: Insights and Advice from Secondary Teachers and Professors.*